IN TIME OF NEED
READING · MEDITATION · PRAYER

W. R. Mackay

THE KNOX PRESS [EDINBURGH]

THE KNOX PRESS [EDINBURGH]
15 North Bank Street, Edinburgh EH1 2LS

© *William R. Mackay*

First published 1966
Reprinted 1972
This revised edition 1989

ISBN 0 904422 03 8

Printed and bound in Great Britain by
McCorquodale (Scotland) Ltd.

Preface

The following selection of daily readings and meditations was not originally intended for publication, but was shared with unseen audiences in the Royal Northern Infirmary and Raigmore Hospital. Patients listened each morning on the headphones by their beds to a relay of 'Morning Prayers' from the Tweedmouth Memorial Chapel.

Many patients have been kind enough to say that they received help from these morning broadcasts and expressed the wish that they might appear in booklet form. Accordingly they were published in 1966, substantially as they were delivered, and were reprinted several years later.

When the matter of a third edition was mooted it was suggested that it might be helpful if a brief prayer was appended to each meditation and this has been done. It is not intended that these prayers should be a substitute for those which are offered up daily by many who may read this booklet. Rather they are included in the hope that they may initiate and encourage the habit of regular communication with God through prayer on the part of many others, so that they may prove the truth of his promise: 'Draw nigh to God and he will draw nigh to you'.

My thanks are due to the Publications Department of the Free Church of Scotland, to Mr Alastair Morrison, who contributed the foreword to the first edition, and to Miss Kay Maciver, who typed the manuscript of the prayers.

W. R. MACKAY
May 1989

Foreword

Since the inception of the National Health Service the place of the Chaplain in the Hospital Service has become firmly established. In the past it was not always recognised that there was such a close link between the physical and spiritual needs of the patient, but in recent times the fact that man cannot live by bread alone, or for that matter by antibiotics, or even by skilful surgery, has become more widely accepted. It is for this reason that one welcomes this timely publication *In Time of Need*.

The author has a deep insight into the spiritual problems which assail the patient lying in a hospital bed, and in this series of brief devotional talks he brings his readers face to face with what the Word of God has to say by way of comfort and encouragement to all those who are worried and anxious, and he directs them to the God of all comfort whose grace is sufficient for all need.

I am sure the contents of this book will prove to be a source of blessing and consolation to many in time of need.

ALASTAIR MORRISON
Consultant Orthopaedic Surgeon
Raigmore Hospital
Inverness

1

Waiting upon God

READING

I wait for God, my soul doth wait
My hope is in his word,
More than they that for morning watch,
My soul waits for the Lord.

The eyes of all wait upon thee; and thou givest them their meat in due season. Thou openest thy hand and satisfiest the desire of every living thing.

Thou preparest a table before me in the presence of mine enemies, thou anointest my head with oil; my cup runneth over.

And when it was evening his disciples came to him, saying, This is a desert place, and the time is now past; send the multitude away, that they may go into the villages, and buy themselves victuals. But Jesus said unto them, They need not depart; give ye them to eat. And they say unto him, We have here but five loaves, and two fishes. He said, Bring them hither to me. And he commanded the multitude to sit down on the grass, and took the five loaves and the two fishes, and looking up to heaven, he blessed, and brake, and gave the loaves to his disciples, and the disciples to the multitude. And they did all eat and were filled; and they took up of the fragments that remained twelve baskets full.

For we brought nothing into this world and it is certain we can carry nothing out. And having food and raiment let us be therewith content.

PSALM 145: 15-16	MATTHEW 14: 15-20
PSALM 23: 5	1 TIMOTHY 6: 7-8

MEDITATION

There are so many things we take for granted that it is only when we are denied them that we appreciate their value. This is especially true of health and strength. How seldom we remember that they form part of the provision which God makes continually so that we may engage in the activities of life! But when God sees fit to deny us temporarily our usual vigour of mind and body, this does not mean to say that He no longer cares or that His provision has ceased. He makes provision for days of sickness as well as for days of health, and to this many of us can testify. Above all, sickness can be a blessing in disguise, for it gives us time to think of God and to wait upon God, and 'they that wait upon the Lord shall renew their strength; they shall mount up with wings as eagles, they shall run and not be weary, and they shall walk and not faint'.

> *Mere human power shall fast decay*
> *And youthful vigour cease*
> *But they who wait upon the Lord*
> *In strength shall still increase.*

> *On eagles' wings they mount, they soar,*
> *Their wings are faith and love,*
> *Till, past the cloudy regions here,*
> *They rise to heaven above.*

PRAYER

Thou knowest O Lord how insufficient we often feel as we seek to cope with the problems and trials of this present life. Help us as we bow before Thee at this time to claim Thy promise of new strength so that on eagles' wings we may be able to soar above the material things of this life and receive new strength as we wait upon Thee. We ask this through Jesus Christ our Lord.

AMEN.

2

The Word of God

READING

Thy word for ever is, O Lord
In heaven settled fast;
Unto all generations
Thy faithfulness doth last.

The Lord gave the word; great was the company of those that published it.

Thy word is a lamp unto my feet and a light unto my path.

Now ye are clean through the word which I have spoken unto you.

Jesus answered and said unto him, If a man love me he will keep my words and my Father will love him and we will come unto him and make our abode with him. He that loveth me not keepeth not my sayings and the word which ye hear is not mine but the Father's which sent me.

For if the word spoken by angels was steadfast and every transgression and disobedience received a just recompense of reward; how shall we escape if we neglect so great salvation.

Wherefore . . . receive with meekness the engrafted word which is able to save your souls. But be ye doers of the word and not hearers only, deceiving your own selves.

PSALM 68: 11	JOHN 14: 23-24
PSALM 119: 105	HEBREWS 2: 2-3
JOHN 15: 3	JAMES 1: 21-22

MEDITATION

We call the Bible the Word of God because we believe that God speaks to us through its pages—'Holy men of God spake as they were moved by the Holy Ghost'. Now God has promised that His Word shall not return unto Him void, and if we want proof of that we find it in transformed lives. The Bible does something for men which no other book can do; it brings them courage, strength, cheer, hope; most important of all it brings salvation—'to you', says Paul, 'the word of this salvation has been sent'. Moreover our attitude to the Word of God reveals what kind of men we are—'whoso keepeth his word in him verily is the love of God perfected; hereby know we that we are in him'. Let us ask ourselves then, in the silence of this hour, whether the Word of God is found dwelling in our hearts.

Lord, Thy Word abideth,
And our footsteps guideth,
Who its truth believeth,
Light and joy receiveth.

O that we, discerning,
Its most holy learning,
Lord, may love and fear Thee,
Evermore be near Thee.

PRAYER

O Lord, we praise Thee today for Thy Word which Thou hast given to us to be a lamp unto our feet and a light unto our path. As we read it may it bring us comfort, hope and encouragement, and through the enlightenment of the Holy Spirit, may it speak to our hearts, and may we be enabled to practise it in our lives, for Jesus' sake.

AMEN.

3

In Time of Need

READING

God is our refuge and our strength,
In straits a present aid;
Therefore, although the earth remove,
We will not be afraid.

They that are whole need not a physician but they that are sick.

Let us therefore come boldly unto the throne of grace, that we may obtain mercy and find grace to help in time of need.

Thou art my hiding place and my shield. I hope in thy word.

And a man shall be as an hiding place from the wind, and a covert from the tempest; as rivers of water in a dry place, as the shadow of a great rock in a weary land.

He that dwelleth in the secret place of the most High shall abide under the shadow of the Almighty. I will say of the Lord, He is my refuge and my fortress: my God; in him will I trust. Surely he shall deliver thee from the snare of the fowler, and from the noisome pestilence. He shall cover thee with his feathers, and under his wings shalt thou trust: His truth shall be thy shield and buckler.

One thing have I desired of the Lord, that will I seek after; that I may dwell in the house of the Lord all the days of my life, to behold the beauty of the Lord, and to enquire in his temple. For in the time of trouble he shall hide me in his pavilion; in the secret of his tabernacle shall he hide me; He shall set me up upon a rock.

LUKE 5: 31	ISAIAH 32: 2
HEBREWS 4: 16	PSALM 91: 1-4
PSALM 119: 114	PSALM 27: 4-5

MEDITATION

'God is a very present help in trouble'. I wonder if you have ever realised that? We so often think of God as One who is far off, but we must remember that He is also close at hand, and His ear is ever open to hear our cry. 'Call upon me in the day of trouble', He has said, 'and I will answer thee'. But have you done that? When did you last pray? Do I hear somebody saying, 'Oh, it is so long ago that I cannot remember'. Well then, this is your time of trouble and God is waiting to hear you cry and if you call upon Him He will honour His promise, for He never fails. So let us bow before Him in humble penitence and faith seeking that blessing which we so much need and which He alone can provide.

Come, let us to the Lord our God
With contrite hearts return;
Our God is gracious nor will leave
The desolate to mourn.

So shall his presence bless our souls,
And shed a joyful light:
That hallow'd morn shall chase away
The sorrows of the night.

PRAYER

Most gracious God, who art a very present help in trouble, and who hast told us to draw near to Thee in time of need; speak to us in the stillness of this hour; bless to us all the dispensations of Thy Providence so that they may serve to draw us closer to Thyself, and make us to realise our total dependence on Thee, through Jesus Christ our Lord.

AMEN

4

Thanksgiving

READING

Praise God for he is kind:
His mercy lasts for aye.
Give thanks with heart and mind
To God of gods alway.
For certainly his mercies dure
Most firm and sure
Eternally.

It is a good thing to give thanks unto the Lord.

Praise ye the Lord. O give thanks unto the Lord; for he is good: for his mercy endureth for ever.

Enter into his gates with thanksgiving, and into his courts with praise: be thankful unto him, and bless his name.

For the Lord is good; his mercy is everlasting; and his truth endureth to all generations.

Bless the Lord, O my soul: and all that is within me, bless his holy name. Bless the Lord, O my soul, and forget not all his benefits: who forgiveth all thine iniquities: who healeth all thy disease; who redeemeth thy life from destruction; who crowneth thee with loving kindness and tender mercies.

Oh that men would praise the Lord for his goodness, and for his wonderful works to the children of men! For he satisfieth the longing soul, and filleth the hungry soul with goodness.

PSALM 92: 1	PSALM 103: 1-4
PSALM 106: 1	PSALM 107: 8-9
PSALM 100: 4-5	

MEDITATION

It is such an easy matter to say *thank you*, and probably for that reason we seldom forget this little courtesy when we receive some service from our fellows. Yet how often we forget to say thank you to the greatest benefactor of all; in fact we find it much easier to complain. When the least little thing happens to upset the even tenor of our lives, we are so ready to grumble and grouse while all the time we forget the many blessings which we receive each day from the hand of God. Let us try for a change to count our blessings rather than our troubles, and when we do this it will indeed surprise us to find how much we have to praise God for, and our troubles will be all the easier to bear, especially if we remember that even troubles can be blessings in disguise.

Now thank we all our God,
With heart and hands and voices,
Who wondrous things hath done,
In whom His world rejoices,
Who, from our mother's arms,
Hath blessed us on our way,
With countless gifts of love,
And still is ours today.

PRAYER

We confess with shame O Lord that while Thou art ever mindful of us we are often forgetful of Thee. Forgive us O Lord for our lack of gratitude and help us to praise Thee for all Thy gifts and especially for the gift of Thy dear Son, who for the salvation of men suffered and died upon the Cross. Help us today to rest on the sufficiency of His sacrifice. We ask this in His Name and for His sake.

AMEN.

5

Anxiety

READING

Cast thou thy burden on the Lord
And he shall thee sustain;
Yea, he shall cause the righteous man
Unmoved to remain.

Therefore I say unto you. Take no thought for your life, what ye shall eat, or what ye shall drink; nor yet for your body what ye shall put on. Is not the life more than meat and the body than raiment? Behold the fowls of the air, for they sow not, neither do they reap, nor gather into barns; yet your heavenly Father feedeth them. And why take ye thought for raiment? Consider the lilies of the field, how they grow, they toil not, neither do they spin: and yet I say unto you, that even Solomon in all his glory was not arrayed like one of these. Wherefore, if God so clothe the grass of the field, which today is, and tomorrow is cast into the oven, shall he not much more clothe you, O ye of little faith? Therefore take no thought, saying what shall we eat? or what shall we drink? or wherewithall shall we be clothed? for your heavenly Father knoweth that ye have need of all these things. But seek ye first the Kingdom of God, and his righteousness; and all these things shall be added unto you. Take therefore no thought for the morrow; for the morrow shall take thought for the things of itself. Sufficient unto the day is the evil thereof.

Be careful for nothing, but in everything by prayer and supplication with thanksgiving let your requests be made known unto God.

Casting all your care upon him; for he careth for you.

MATTHEW 6: 25, 26, 28-34   1 PETER 5: 7
PHILIPPIANS 4: 6

MEDITATION

There are a great many lonely souls in the world and what a difference it would make to them if they only felt that there was someone who cared for them, one to whom they could bring their burdens and their difficulties. Yet if only they realised it, there is such a One—there is 'a Friend that sticketh closer than a brother'.

In Jesus Christ we have a Friend who, not only is willing to hear our cry in time of need, but who, because of the resources which He commands, is able to bring us succour and help at all times, and in all circumstances. Yet, strange though it may seem, all too often we are found bearing our own burdens, and life becomes a misery. So let us bring to Him the burdens which chafe our shoulders, and the cares and anxieties which weigh us down. Above all, let us bring to Him the heaviest burden of all, namely, the burden of our sins, remembering that He is the great Burden Bearer: 'Who his own self bare our sins in his own body on the tree.'

> *All your anxiety, all your care*
> *Bring to the mercy seat, leave it there,*
> *Never a burden He cannot bear,*
> *Never a Friend like Jesus.*

PRAYER

Our gracious God and Father, we remember before Thee all who are bearing heavy burdens and commend them to Thy loving tender care. In their hour of loneliness and anxiety may they know the companionship of the Heavenly Friend, and, casting their every burden upon Him may they be sustained and upheld by the strong arm of Almighty Love. We ask this through Jesus Christ our Lord.

AMEN.

6

Wisdom

READING

Wisdom's beginning is God's fear:
Good understanding they
Have all that His commands fulfil:
His praise endures for aye.

Happy is the man that findeth wisdom, and the man that getteth understanding. For the merchandise of it is better than the merchandise of silver, and the gain thereof than fine gold. She is more precious than rubies; and all the things thou canst desire are not to be compared unto her. Length of days is in her right hand; and in her left hand riches and honour. Her ways are ways of pleasantness, and all her paths are peace. She is a tree of life to them that lay hold upon her; and happy is every one that retaineth her. The Lord by wisdom hath founded the earth, by understanding hath he established the heavens. By his knowledge the depths are broken up, and the clouds drop down the dew.

Get wisdom, get understanding; forget it not; neither decline from the words of my mouth. Forsake her not, and she shall preserve thee; Love her, and she shall keep thee. Wisdom is the principal thing; therefore get wisdom; and with all thy getting get understanding. Exalt her, and she shall promote thee; she shall bring thee to honour, when thou dost embrace her. She shall give to thine head an ornament of grace; a crown of Glory shall she deliver to thee. Hear, O my son and receive my sayings, and the years of thy life shall be many.

PROVERBS 3: 13-20   PROVERBS 4: 5-10

MEDITATION

When Solomon was asked what gift he would like from God, he did not ask for wealth or power or popularity, but he requested that he might be given wisdom and God commended him for his choice. So here, drawing no doubt upon his own experience, he writes 'happy is the man that findeth wisdom'. It is well for us to remember, however, that there is a difference between the wisdom of this world and that wisdom which is commended in Scripture. It is possible to be worldly wise and yet ignorant regarding spiritual values—'the wisdom of this world is foolishness with God'. What we are called upon to do, therefore, is to cultivate true wisdom, that wisdom whereby we see ourselves as needy creatures, that wisdom whereby in faith we are 'enabled to embrace Jesus Christ as he is freely offered in the Gospel'. Wherefore 'get wisdom, get understanding'.

> *O happy is the man who hears, instruction's warning voice;*
> *And who celestial Wisdom makes his early, only choice,*
> *For she has treasures greater far than east or west unfold;*
> *And her rewards more precious are, than all their stores of*
> *gold.*

PRAYER

O Lord, who art the fount of all knowledge and the source of all wisdom, help us to find that true wisdom which shall enable us to see things in their true perspective. May we seek first the kingdom of God and His righteousness, and ever journeying onward in His strength and by His grace go from strength to strength unwearied until at length we appear before Him. In Christ's name we ask this.

AMEN.

7

Jesus Christ is Lord

READING

Ye gates, lift up your heads on high;
Ye doors that last for aye,
Be lifted up, that so the King
Of glory enter may.

I have sworn by myself, the word is gone out of my mouth in righteousness, and shall not return, That unto me every knee shall bow, every tongue shall swear.

But now we see not yet all things put under him. But we see Jesus, who was made a little lower than the angels for the suffering of death, crowned with glory and honour; that he by the grace of God should taste death for every man. For it became him, for whom are all things, and by whom are all things, in bringing many sons unto glory, to make the captain of their salvation perfect through sufferings.

Let this mind be in you, which was also in Christ Jesus; who, being in the form of God, thought it not robbery to be equal with God; but made himself of no reputation, and took upon him the form of a servant, and was made in the likeness of men; and being found in fashion, as a man, he humbled himself, and became obedient unto death, even the death of the cross. Wherefore God also hath highly exalted him, and given him a name which is above every name; that at the name of Jesus every knee should bow, of things in heaven, and things in earth; and things under the earth; and that every tongue should confess that Jesus Christ is Lord, to the glory of God the Father.

ISAIAH 45: 23   PHILIPPIANS 2: 5-11
HEBREWS 2: 8-10

MEDITATION

One of the troubles with much of our religion at the present day is that Jesus Christ is not given his rightful place. True, He is acknowledged as a great historical figure, a great Teacher and Healer, whose example we would do well to follow. But He is more than that—He is Saviour and Lord. Jesus Christ is the Son of God, the One who for the salvation of men humbled himself and became obedient unto death, even the death of the Cross. This same Jesus has now risen in mighty and triumphant power. Wherefore we read 'God hath highly exalted him ... that at the name of Jesus every knee should bow and every tongue confess that Jesus Christ is Lord'. Yet how sad it is to remember that there are many who have never confessed Jesus Christ as Lord and who have never acknowledged their indebtedness to Him for all that He has done. Where do you stand in this matter? Is Jesus Christ Lord of your life? Now that you have time to think about these things will you face up to this great question for it is tremendously important?

Thy kingdom come, O God
Thy rule, O Christ, begin
Break with Thine iron rod
The tyrannies of sin.

PRAYER

We give Thee thanks O Lord for Jesus Christ Thy Son who lived among men and who died for men. We rejoice that He has now risen in mighty and victorious power. Give us faith we pray to claim Him as our Lord and Saviour and to rejoice in that hope which He brings to us through the triumph of His resurrection.

AMEN.

The Kingdom of God

READING

Thy kingdom hath none end at all,
It doth through ages all remain.
The Lord upholdeth all that fall,
The cast-down raiseth up again.

All the ends of the earth shall remember and turn unto the Lord; and all the kindreds of the nations shall worship before thee. For the kingdom is the Lord's and he is the governor among the nations.

For the kingdom of God is not meat and drink; but righteousness, and peace, and joy in the Holy Ghost. For he that in these things serveth Christ is acceptable to God and approved of men.

Not everyone that saith unto me Lord, Lord, shall enter into the kingdom of heaven; but he that doeth the will of my Father which is in heaven.

Verily, verily, I say unto thee, Except a man be born again he cannot see the kingdom of God.

No man having put his hand to the plough and looking back, is fit for the kingdom of God.

Wherefore the rather, brethren, give diligence to make your calling and election sure; for if ye do these things, ye shall never fall: For so an entrance shall be ministered unto you abundantly into the everlasting kingdom of our Lord and Saviour Jesus Christ.

PSALM 22: 27-28	JOHN 3: 3, 2
ROMANS 14: 17-18	LUKE 9: 62
MATTHEW 7: 21	2 PETER 1: 10-11.

MEDITATION

For a time the disciples of Jesus were under the misapprehension that he was going to set up a kingdom on this earth and they no doubt thought that when this kingdom was set up they would occupy positions of authority and responsibility. It came as a tremendous shock to them, therefore, when they saw their Lord and Master crucified upon a cross of shame. Yet Jesus had continually told them that His kingdom was not of this world; it was a spiritual kingdom—a kingdom which He was to set up within the hearts of men and women. Thus when Nicodemus came to Him He said, 'except a man be born again he cannot see the kingdom of God'.

The kingdom of God may be said to be set up whenever a heart by God's grace is opened to receive Him; and when Jesus Christ reigns within the heart and life it brings new hope, new strength, and a feeling of peace and joy no matter what experiences we may be called upon to pass through. How important then that we should open the doors of our hearts to receive Him so that this hope and joy may be ours!

> *Jesus shall reign where'er the sun*
> *Does his successive journeys run;*
> *His Kingdom stretch from shore to shore,*
> *Till moons shall wax and wane no more.*

PRAYER

Eternal and ever blessed Lord, who art the supreme ruler of the universe and who dost set up Thy kingdom in every contrite heart, open our hearts by Thy grace we beseech of Thee so that the King of Glory may come in. May we take our place as little children before Thee so that entering into the kingdom of God we shall praise Thee not only in this present life but throughout the countless ages of eternity. We ask this for Jesus' sake.

AMEN.

9

Christian Warfare

READING

Thy sword gird on thy thigh
Thou that art most of might:
Appear in dreadful majesty,
And in thy glory bright.

Fight the good fight of faith, lay hold on eternal life, whereunto thou are also called, and hast professed a good profession before many witnesses.

Be strong in the Lord, and in the power of his might. Put on the whole armour of God, that ye may be able to stand against the wiles of the devil. For we wrestle, not against flesh and blood, but against principalities, against powers, against the rulers of the darkness of this world, against spiritual wickedness in high places. Wherefore take unto you the whole armour of God, that ye may be able to withstand in the evil day, and having done all to stand. Stand, therefore, having your loins girt about with truth, and having on the breastplate of righteousness; and your feet shod with the preparation of the gospel of peace; above all, taking the shield of faith, wherewith ye shall be able to quench all the fiery darts of the wicked. And take the helmet of salvation, and the sword of the Spirit, which is the word of God.

1 TIMOTHY 6: 12   EPHESIANS 6: 10-17

MEDITATION

'Put on the whole armour of God'. This is the language of
the battlefield. It is the voice of a commander summoning
his troops to action and reminding them of the necessity of
being properly equipped as they go forth to meet the
enemy. The Christian life is a continual warfare and too
often we have to admit defeat as we wage war against the
evil in our own hearts and in the world around. Our defeat
may be due to the fact that we have been relying on our
own resources and the forces of evil have been too strong
for us. Let us 'put on the whole armour of God'
remembering that His strength is made perfect in our
weakness and that 'the victory which overcometh the
world' is our faith.

> *Soldiers of Christ, arise*
> *And put your armour on,*
> *Strong in the strength which God supplies*
> *Through His eternal Son;*
> *Strong in the Lord of Hosts,*
> *And in His mighty power,*
> *Who in the strength of Jesus trusts*
> *Is more than conqueror.*

PRAYER

O Thou who art the Captain of our salvation and who
hast provided for us the whole armour of God with which
to fight against the forces of evil in the world around us,
help us to fight the good fight of faith and to endure
hardness as good soldiers of Jesus Christ so that when the
last battle is over we may wear the victor's crown and live
with Thee for ever in Thy kingdom.

AMEN.

The Presence of God

READING

Then at God's presence shook the earth,
Then drops from heaven fell;
This Sinai shook before the Lord,
The God of Israel.

I am troubled at his presence.

Whither shall I go from thy spirit? or whither shall I flee from thy presence? If I ascend up into heaven thou art there: if I make my bed in hell, behold, thou art there. If I take the wings of the morning and dwell in the uttermost parts of the sea, even there shall thy hand lead me and thy right hand shall hold me. If I say, Surely the darkness shall cover me; even the night shall be light about me. Yea, the darkness hideth not from thee, but the night shineth as the day; the darkness and the light are both alike to thee.

The Lord of Hosts is with us; the God of Jacob is our refuge.

My presence shall go with thee, and I will give thee rest.

Repent ye therefore and be converted, that your sins may be blotted out, when the times of refreshing shall come from the presence of the Lord.

JOB 23: 15   EXODUS 33: 14
PSALM 139: 7-12   ACTS 3: 19
PSALM 46: 7

MEDITATION

Paradoxical though it may seem the realisation of God's Presence can do two things to men—it can make them afraid or it can promote a sense of security. It makes men afraid because they realise that their sinful nature cannot bear the scrutiny of God's eye, and they realise too that they cannot place themselves outwith God's scrutiny, for His eye is ever on them. Yet how comforting it can be to remind ourselves that God's eye is upon us, for it assures us that He knows our every weakness and our every anxiety. And has He not said 'when thou passest through the waters I will be with thee; and through the rivers, they shall not overflow thee'? So let us pray for a realisation of God's Presence today in order that it may serve as an antidote both to sin and to fear.

Redeemer come! I open wide
My heart to Thee; here Lord abide
Let me Thy inner presence feel
Thy grace and love in me reveal.

PRAYER

O Lord as we bow before Thee help us to remember that although we cannot see Thee with the natural eye yet we believe that Thou art here for Thou art the omnipresent One. May that assurance of Thy Presence bring us comfort and hope and joy, and may the awareness of Thy Presence constrain us when we are tempted to sin against Thee. We ask this through Jesus Christ our Lord.

AMEN.

11

The Christian Hope

READING

My soul, wait thou with patience
Upon thy God alone;
On him dependeth all my hope
And expectation.

Blessed is the man that trusteth in the Lord and whose hope the Lord is.

Happy is he that hath the God of Jacob for his help, whose help is in the Lord his God.

The hope of the righteous shall be gladness but the expectation of the wicked shall perish.

And now Lord what wait I for? my hope is in thee.

Uphold me according unto thy word, that I may live, and let me not be ashamed of my hope.

For whatsoever things were written aforetime were written for our learning, that we through patience and comfort of the scripture might have hope.

For we are saved by hope; but hope that is seen is not hope; for what a man seeth, why doth he yet hope for? But if we hope for what we see not, then do we with patience wait for it.

Be not moved away from the hope of the gospel, which ye have heard and which was preached to every creature which is under heaven.

JEREMIAH 17: 7	PSALM 119: 116
PSALM 146: 5	ROMANS 15: 4
PROVERBS 10: 28	ROMANS 8: 24-25
PSALM 39: 7	COLOSSIANS 1: 23

MEDITATION

'Hope' we read 'springs eternal in the human breast' and this world would be a poor place without hope. We hope that today's sadness is going to be replaced by tomorrow's gladness, today's illness by tomorrow's health, and today's adversity by tomorrow's prosperity. Unfortunately, however, our hope is sometimes little better than wishful thinking because we have little or no ground for believing that it will be realised. The Christian hope, by contrast, is entirely different for it is built upon a firm foundation, namely on the great certainty that Jesus died and rose again, and we have the sure promise that if we commit our way unto Him then all shall be well. May ours be the hope which shall enable us to say:

> *I know that safe with Him remains,*
> *Protected by his power,*
> *What I've committed to his trust,*
> *Till the decisive hour.*
>
> *Then will He own His servant's name*
> *Before His Father's face,*
> *And in the New Jerusalem*
> *Appoint my soul a place.*

PRAYER

We praise Thee O Lord for the Christian hope and for all that it means to us as we journey on through life's perplexing paths. Help us to remember that it is built upon a sure foundation and that it is a hope of which we need never be ashamed for it is an anchor cast within the veil. May that hope be ours today through Jesus Christ our Lord.

AMEN.

12

The Heavenly Friend

READING

Hear Lord my prayer; unto the voice
Of my request attend:
In troublous times I'll call on thee;
For thou wilt answer send.

And the Lord spake unto Moses face to face, as a man speaketh unto his friend.

A friend loveth at all times, and a brother is born for adversity.

Faithful are the wounds of a friend, but the kisses of an enemy are deceitful. Ointment and perfume rejoice the heart, so doth the sweetness of a man's friend by hearty counsel. Iron sharpeneth iron; so a man sharpeneth the countenance of his friend.

A man that hath friends must show himself friendly; and there is a friend that sticketh closer than a brother.

Greater love hath no man than this, that a man lay down his life for his friends. Ye are my friends, if ye do whatsoever I command you. Henceforth I call you not servants; for the servant knoweth not what his Lord doeth; but I have called you friends; for all things that I have heard of my Father I have made known unto you.

EXODUS 33: 11
PROVERBS 17: 17
PROVERBS 27: 6, 9, 17

PROVERBS 18: 24
JOHN 15: 13-15

MEDITATION

Friendship is one of those blessings which sweetens the relationships of life and fortunate indeed is the man who in his hour of need has a friend to whom he can turn, knowing full well that that friend will help him to the limit of his resources. Now it is just at this point that the friendship of Jesus Christ surpasses every human friendship because He commands the storehouses of Heaven and earth and there are no bounds to the help which He can give. Moreover, He is a faithful and true friend in that He points out to us our failures and our wrong doing, and above all His love and concern have been made manifest by His dying for our sins on the Cross of Calvary. How do you treat this friend? Is He a welcome guest in your heart and in your home or is He still standing outside?

What a Friend we have in Jesus,
All our sins and griefs to bear!
What a privilege to carry
Everything to God in prayer!

O what peace we often forfeit,
O what needless pain we bear,
All because we do not carry
Everything to God in prayer!

PRAYER

O Lord, who hast set the solitary in families, we give Thee thanks today for our loved ones, and our friends. We thank Thee for all that they mean to us, and for all they do for us, but we thank Thee especially for the heavenly Friend whose love was manifested on the Cross of Calvary. As we are reminded anew today of the wonder of His love may we be able to say humbly and reverently 'We love Him because He first loved us.' We ask this through Jesus Christ our Lord.   AMEN.

The Bread of Life

READING

For thirst and hunger in them faints
Their soul; when straits them press,
They cry unto the Lord, and he
Them frees from their distress.

Wherefore do ye spend money for that which is not bread? and your labour for that which satisfieth not? hearken diligently unto me and eat ye that which is good and let your soul delight itself in fatness.

For the bread of God is he which cometh down from heaven and giveth life unto the world. Then said they unto him, Lord, evermore give us this bread. And Jesus said unto them, I am the bread of life, he that cometh to me shall never hunger; verily, verily, I say unto you, He that believeth in me hath everlasting life. I am that bread of life. Your fathers did eat manna in the wilderness and are dead. This is the bread which cometh down from heaven that a man may eat thereof and not die. I am the living bread which came down from heaven; if any man eat of this bread, he shall live for ever; and the bread that I will give is my flesh, which I will give for the life of the world.

The bread which we break, is it not the communion of the body of Christ? For we being many are one bread and one body, for we are all partakers of that one bread.

ISAIAH 55: 2   1 CORINTHIANS 10: 16-17
JOHN 6: 33-35, 47-51

MEDITATION

'Man shall not live by bread alone'. So spake Jesus when he was tempted by the devil and His words remind us that material things of themselves are not enough. It is not sufficient that our bodies should be well nourished or that we should possess wealth or enjoy popularity. These things may bring a certain amount of satisfaction but they can never satisfy the inner yearning of the soul. God, however, has made provision whereby hungry souls can be fed and Jesus Christ is graphically described as the Bread of Life. That means that just as food satisfies our physical needs so Christ satisfies our spiritual needs. So let us wait upon Him for our spiritual food each day and pray—

> *Break Thou the bread of life,*
> *Dear Lord to me,*
> *As Thou didst break the loaves,*
> *Beside the sea.*
>
> *Beyond the sacred page*
> *I seek Thee, Lord;*
> *My spirit pants for Thee,*
> *O living Word.*

PRAYER

Most gracious God who gives bread to the hungry and water to the thirsty and who provides for all our recurring needs, grant that we may ever remember that man shall not live by bread alone but by every word which proceeds out of the mouth of God. Help us each day to feed upon that living bread so that nourished and strengthened thereby we may be able to witness to Thy love and to Thy power before our fellows, for Christ's sake.

AMEN.

14

Water for the Thirsty

READING

Like as the hart for water brooks
In thirst doth pant and bray;
So pants my longing soul, O God,
That come to thee I may.

Now Jacob's well was there. Jesus, therefore, being wearied with his journey sat thus on the well; and it was about the sixth hour. There cometh a woman of Samaria to draw water: Jesus saith unto her, Give me to drink. Then saith the woman of Samaria unto him, How is it that thou, being a Jew, asketh drink of me, which am a woman of Samaria? for the Jews have no dealings with the Samaritans. Jesus answered and said unto her, If thou knewest the gift of God, and who it is that saith to thee, Give me to drink, thou wouldest have asked of him, and he would have given thee living water. The woman saith unto him, Sir thou hast nothing to draw with and the well is deep; from whence has thou that living water? Art thou greater than our father Jacob, which gave us the well, and drank thereof himself and his children and his cattle? Jesus answered and said unto her, Whosoever drinketh of this water shall thirst again. But whosoever drinketh of the water that I shall give him shall never thirst, but the water that I shall give him shall be in him a well of water springing up into everlasting life. The woman saith unto him, Sir, give me this water that I thirst not, neither come hither to draw.

JOHN 4: 6-15

MEDITATION

What a demanding thing thirst is and its demands remain insistent until it is satisfied. Even Jesus Christ himself knew what it meant to be thirsty and he requested a drink from a woman of Samaria. At the same time he taught her a great lesson: 'Whosoever', he said, 'drinketh of this water shall thirst again, but whosoever drinketh of the water that I shall give him shall never thirst'. How many people there are who seek to quench their thirst—whether it be a thirst for excitement, or happiness, or satisfaction—at the cisterns of this world only to find that each time they return their sense of enjoyment is diminished! Their experience may be summed up in the words of the hymn writer—

I tried the broken cisterns Lord,
But, ah, the waters failed,
Even as I stooped to drink they fled,
And mocked me as I wailed.

How different it is with those who partake of the living water which Christ offers, for having done so they confess—

Now none but Christ can satisfy,
No other name for me,
There's love and life and lasting joy,
Lord Jesus found in thee.

PRAYER

We confess with shame O Lord that too often we are found thirsting after those things which can never satisfy and so we pray that Thou wouldest create within us a thirst after Thyself. Give us O Lord a drink of that living water of which Thou hast said that 'if any man drink he shall never thirst again'. And thus refreshed and re-invigorated may we journey along the pilgrim way until by Thy grace we reach that place where we shall hunger no more, neither thirst any more. And this we ask for Christ's sake.

AMEN.

15

Humility

For thou a little lower hast
Him that the angels made;
With glory and with dignity
Thou crowned hast his head.

Wherewith shall I come before the Lord, and bow myself before the high God?

For thus saith the high and lofty one that inhabiteth eternity, whose name is holy, I dwell in the high and holy place, with him also that is of a contrite and humble spirit.

And Jesus called a little child unto him, and set him in the midst of them, and said, Verily I say unto you, Except ye be converted and become as little children, ye shall not enter into the kingdom of heaven. Whosover therefore shall humble himself as this little child the same is greatest in the kingdom of heaven.

For whosoever exalteth himself shall be abased; and he that humbleth himself shall be exalted.

Let this mind be in you which was also in Christ Jesus: who, being in the form of God, thought it not robbery to be equal with God; but made himself of no reputation, and took upon him the form of a servant, and was made in the likeness of men: and being found in fashion as a man, he humbled himself and became obedient unto death, even the death of the cross. Wherefore God also hath highly exalted him and given him a name which is above every name.

Humble yourselves therefore under the mighty hand of God, that he may exalt you in due time.

MICAH 6: 6	LUKE 14: 11
ISAIAH 57: 15	PHILIPPIANS 2: 5-9
MATTHEW 18: 2-4	1 PETER 5: 6

MEDITATION

There are few graces more beautiful than humility, and yet how few there are who attain to it. Pride is something which is part of our human nature and consequently we do not like to think that we cannot justify ourselves. Yet God has said 'except ye become as little children ye shall in no wise enter the kingdom of heaven'. If you think that that is something which is too hard for you, then remember what the Son of God did: 'he who thought it not robbery to be equal with God humbled himself and became obedient unto death'. So let us humble ourselves in His Presence remembering that if we do He shall exalt us.

Oh for a heart to praise my God,
A heart from sin set free,
A heart that's sprinkled with the blood
So freely shed for me.

A humble, lowly, contrite heart
Believing, true and clean
Which neither life nor death can part
From Him that dwells within.

PRAYER

Rebuke our proud hearts we beseech Thee O Lord and help us to come into Thy Presence in the spirit of reverence and humility remembering that we are sinners both by nature and practice. May we take our place as little children at Thy feet remembering that unless we do we shall not enter the kingdom of heaven. Enable us to seek first the kingdom of God and His righteousness and to journey ever onward until our travelling days are done. We ask this through Jesus Christ our Lord.

AMEN.

16

Forgiveness

READING

For thou art gracious, O Lord,
And ready to forgive;
And rich in mercy, all that call
Upon thee to relieve.

Who is a God like unto thee, that pardoneth iniquity, and passeth by the transgression of the remnant of his heritage? He retaineth not his anger for ever because he delighteth in mercy.

The Lord is merciful and gracious, slow to anger, and plenteous in mercy. He will not always chide: neither will he keep his anger forever. He hath not dealt with us after our sins; nor rewarded us according to our iniquities. For as the heaven is high above the earth, so great is his mercy toward them that fear him. As far as the east is from the west, so far hath he removed our transgressions from us. Like as a father pitieth his children, so the Lord pitieth them that fear him.

For thou desirest not sacrifice; else would I give it; thou delightest not in burnt offering. The sacrifices of God are a broken spirit; a broken and a contrite heart. O God, thou wilt not despise.

MICAH 7: 18   PSALM 51: 16-17
PSALM 103: 8-13

MEDITATION

One of the most wonderful things about God is His forgiveness. Despite the fact that men are continually turning their backs upon Him, His mercy and His pardon are still extended to them. In Old Testament times men used to seek the forgiveness of God as the all-sufficient sacrifice has been offered up once and for all in the person of Jesus Christ our Lord. There is, however, a sacrifice which God still accepts and that is the sacrifice of the broken and contrite heart. Let us then confess our sins to Him today and in the spirit of true repentance offer the sacrifice which is well pleasing in His sight.

> *There is a holy sacrifice*
> *Which God in heaven will not despise,*
> *Yea which is precious in his eyes*
> *The contrite heart.*
>
> *Saviour I cast my hopes on Thee;*
> *Such as Thou art I feign would be*
> *In mercy Lord bestow on me*
> *The contrite heart.*

PRAYER

O Lord, who hast assured us that if we confess our sins Thou art faithful and just to forgive our sins, give us we pray Thee contrite hearts so that in the spirit of true penitence we may bow before Thee, and enable us so to order our lives that we may be found as faithful followers of Jesus Christ, in whose name and for whose sake we ask these things.

AMEN.

The Good Shepherd

READING

The Lord's my shepherd, I'll not want.
He makes me down to lie
In pastures green; He leadeth me
The quiet waters by.

All we like sheep have gone astray; we have turned every one to his own way; and the Lord hath laid on him the iniquity of us all.

Verily, verily, I say unto you, He that entereth not by the door into the sheepfold but climbeth up some other way, the same is a thief and a robber. But he that entereth in by the door is the shepherd of the sheep.

I am the good shepherd; the good shepherd giveth his life for the sheep. I am the good shepherd, and know my sheep, and am known of mine. As the Father knoweth me, even so know I the Father; and I lay down my life for the sheep. And other sheep I have, which are not of this fold; them also I must bring, and they shall hear my voice; and there shall be one fold, and one shepherd. Therefore doth my Father love me, because I lay down my life, that I might take it again.

For ye were as sheep going astray; but are now returned unto the shepherd and bishop of your souls.

Isaiah 53: 6   1 Peter 2: 25
John 10: 1-2, 11, 14-17

MEDITATION

'The Lord is my shepherd'. What memories these words bring to us, memories perhaps of childhood days when some of us first learned to lisp them at our mother's knee, or sang them in the church which we attended. A lot of water has flowed under the bridge since then and with the passing of the years many have strayed far from the green pastures. But the Good Shepherd still cares and he who gave His life for the sheep still seeks the wayward and the lost. Who knows but He may be seeking someone who listens to these words today, and that someone might be you. How wonderful if we should hear His voice say even now 'Rejoice with me for I have found my sheep which was lost'.

Lord, Thou hast here Thy ninety and nine;
Are they not enough for Thee?
But the Shepherd made answer, This of Mine
Has wandered away from Me;
And although the road be rough and steep,
I go to the desert to find My sheep.

PRAYER

O Lord our God we give thanks today for the Good Shepherd who gave His life for the sheep. May we today be found numbered among His flock so that each of us can say truly 'The Lord is my shepherd, I shall not want.' Grant we beseech of Thee out of Thy great mercy that goodness and mercy may follow us throughout our lives and that when our earthly race is run we may dwell in the house of the Lord for ever.

AMEN.

18

Love

I love the Lord because my voice
And prayers he did hear.
I while I live will call on him,
Who bowed to me his ear.

Greater love hath no man than this that a man lay down his life for his friends.

But God commendeth his love towards us in that while we were yet sinners, Christ died for us. Much more then, being now justified by his blood we shall be saved from wrath through him.

Forasmuch as ye know that ye were not redeemed with corruptible things, as silver and gold, from your vain conversation received by tradition from your fathers; but with the precious blood of Christ as of a lamb without blemish and without spot; Who verily was foreordained before the foundation of the world, but was manifest in these last times for you.

Herein is love, not that we loved God, but that He loved us, and sent his Son to be the propitiation for our sins.

For God so loved the world, that he gave his only begotten Son, that whosoever believeth in him should not perish, but have everlasting life.

JOHN 15: 13   1 JOHN 4: 10
ROMANS 5: 8-9   JOHN 3:16
1 PETER 1: 18-20

MEDITATION

The test of love is sacrifice, and the supreme test of all is that a man should lay down his life for his friend. But we have just been reading of a love that is greater than that, 'for while we were yet sinners Christ died for us'. I wonder if we have ever appreciated to the full the marvel of God's love? Just think of it! He gave his only begotten Son. Have you ever realised that? If not, then tarry for a moment 'neath the shadow of His Cross and as with the eye of faith we see there God's love in action so may we be able to say from hearts which are filled with gratitude, 'we love him because he first loved us'.

> *O love that wilt not let me go*
> *I rest my weary soul in Thee:*
> *I give Thee back the life I owe,*
> *That in Thine ocean depths its flow*
> *May richer fuller be.*

PRAYER

Our blessed Lord whose love was made manifest upon the Cross of Calvary, where Thou didst offer Thyself as the all-sufficient sacrifice for sin, may we never cease to marvel at the wonder of Thy love and the riches of Thy grace. Grant we beseech Thee that we may be so united by faith to Christ that we may say from our own experience that He is the Son of God who loved me and gave Himself for me. We ask this for His dear name's sake.

AMEN.

The Trial of Faith

READING

Yea though I walk in death's dark vale
Yet will I fear none ill,
For thou art with me, and thy rod
And staff me comfort still.

Now a certain man was sick, named Lazarus, of Bethany, the town of Mary and her sister Martha. (It was that Mary which anointed the Lord with ointment, and wiped his feet with her hair, whose brother Lazarus was sick.) Therefore his sisters sent unto him, saying, Lord, behold, he whom thou lovest is sick. When Jesus heard that, he said, This sickness is not unto death, but for the glory of God, that the Son of God might be glorified thereby. Now Jesus loved Martha, and her sister, and Lazarus. When he had heard therefore that he was sick, he abode two days still in the same place where he was. Then after that saith he to his disciples, Let us go into Judaea again.

Then said Martha unto Jesus, Lord if thou hadst been here my brother had not died. But I know that even now whatsoever thou wilt ask of God, God will give it Thee. Jesus saith unto her, thy brother shall rise again.

JOHN 11: 1-7, 21-23

MEDITATION

When Jesus heard that his friend Lazarus was sick He remained two days in the place where He was. One would have expected that on receiving this news He would have immediately gone to the help of His friend, but instead of that He delayed His coming, and when He finally decided to go to Bethany, Lazarus was already dead. Strange conduct for a friend, you say, and so it would appear to be! Yet there was a purpose behind this delay because when Jesus arrived at the home of Lazarus He performed a notable miracle by raising him from the dead. Let us remember then that if God does not appear immediately to answer our prayers there is probably a good reason behind it, and although we cannot understand or appreciate that reason now, one day we shall learn that it was for our own good and part of God's plan to draw us more closely to himself.

Him from the dead thou brought'st again,
When by His sacred blood,
Confirmed and sealed for evermore,
The eternal covenant stood.

PRAYER

O Lord, who in Thine infinite wisdom dost sometimes see fit to bring days of adversity into our lives, so that the sunshine of Thy love would appear to be blotted out, help us to praise Thee not only for the pleasant experiences in life but also for those which are unpleasant. May every experience be used of Thee to draw us more closely to Thy side and may our faith emerge triumphant, through Jesus Christ our Lord.

AMEN.

20

Peace with God

READING

I'll hear what God the Lord will speak:
To his folk he'll speak peace,
And to his saints; but let them not
Return to foolishness.

O that thou hadst hearkened to my commandments! then had thy peace been as a river, and thy righteousness as the waves of the sea.

Thou wilt keep him in perfect peace whose mind is stayed on thee.

There is no peace, saith my God, to the wicked.

Peace I leave with you, my peace I give unto you; not as the world giveth, give I unto you. Let not your heart be troubled, neither let it be afraid.

For he is our peace who hath made both one, and hath broken down the middle wall of partition between us; and came and preached peace to you which were afar off, and to them that were nigh.

Therefore, being justified by faith, we have peace with God through our Lord Jesus Christ.

Let the peace of God rule in your hearts.

And the peace of God which passeth all understanding, shall keep your hearts and minds through Christ Jesus.

ISAIAH 48: 18	EPHESIANS 2: 14, 17
ISAIAH 26: 3	ROMANS 5: 1
ISAIAH 57: 21	COLOSSIANS 3: 15
JOHN 14: 27	PHILIPPIANS 4: 7

MEDITATION

What a troubled, restless place this world is, and how many hearts there are which are yearning and longing and seeking for peace! Yet this peace which men seek is so elusive that they never seem to find it. They seek for it in the accumulation of wealth, in the achievement of ambition, or in the pursuit of popularity, but somehow or other it always seems to elude their grasp. The reason for this lies in the fact that man is different from the lower creation—he is possessed of a soul and that soul is restless until it finds its rest in God. What man needs therefore is 'peace with God', and that comes only through Jesus Christ who 'made peace through the blood of his Cross'. This peace becomes ours in an act of faith whereby we are able to claim Christ as Lord and Saviour. 'Therefore being justified by faith' says Paul 'we have peace with God through our Lord Jesus Christ'. May we all be able to exercise this faith and enjoy that peace for which we long so much.

> *Stayed upon Jehovah*
> *Hearts are fully blest,*
> *Finding as He promised*
> *Perfect peace and rest.*

PRAYER

Eternal and ever blessed God, who didst bring peace through the blood of Thy Cross, grant that as we journey through this troubled world we may know that deep sweet peace which passes understanding, and even amidst the storms and anxieties of life may we know that all is well if our trust is in Thee; we ask this, with the forgiveness of all our sins, for Christ's sake.

AMEN.

21

Joy

READING

Thou wilt me show the path of life:
Of joys there is full store
Before thy face; at thy right hand
Are pleasures evermore.

The joy of the Lord is your strength.

Cast me not away from thy presence and take not thy Holy Spirit from me. Restore unto me the joy of thy salvation and uphold me with thy free Spirit.

I will rejoice in the Lord, I will joy in the God of my salvation.

I will mention the loving kindnesses of the Lord and the praises of the Lord according to all that the Lord hath bestowed on us and the great goodness toward the house of Israel which he hath bestowed on them according to his mercies and according to the multitude of his loving kindnesses. In all their affliction he was afflicted and the angel of his presence saved them; in his love and in his pity he redeemed them and he bare them and carried them all the days of old.

Repent ye therefore and be converted, that your sins may be blotted out when the times of refreshing shall come from the presence of the Lord.

And the ransomed of the Lord shall return and come to Zion with songs and everlasting joy upon their heads: they shall obtain joy and gladness and sorrow and sighing shall flee away.

NEHEMIAH 8: 10   ISAIAH 63: 7, 9
PSALM 51: 11-12   ACTS 3: 19
HABAKKUK 3: 18   ISAIAH 35: 10

MEDITATION

There are many people who appear to think that religion is dull and uninteresting, and that to be a Christian is to rob life of its joy. Never was there a greater mistake, for there is no joy to be compared with the joy which the Christian possesses and which comes through the knowledge of forgiveness and the hope of eternal life. By comparison, the best which this world has to offer seems poor indeed, and yet how many there are who are trying to content themselves with a happiness which is only temporary and fleeting. The secret of true joy lies in the realisation of Christ's presence and of the sufficiency of His sacrifice. So let us ask for grace today to have our eyes directed towards the Lamb of Calvary and as we behold Him may we be able to say with joy and gladness in our hearts—

My faith looks up to Thee,
Thou Lamb of Calvary,
Saviour Divine:
Now hear me while I pray;
Take all my guilt away;
O let me from this day
Be wholly Thine.

PRAYER

We praise Thy holy name O Lord for all the joy which Thou dost bring into our lives, especially the joy which comes through the knowledge of sins forgiven. Enable us to rejoice today in a Saviour's love and in a Saviour's sacrifice and may the assurance of Thy Presence with us drive out our every fear. We ask this in the precious name of our Lord and Saviour Jesus Christ.

AMEN.

Endurance

READING

His name for ever shall endure;
Last like the sun it shall:
Men shall be blessed in him, and blessed
All nations shall him call.

Can thine heart endure, or can thine hands be strong in the days that I shall deal with thee?

Blessed is the man that endureth temptation for, when he is tried, he shall receive the crown of life; which the Lord hath promised to them that love him.

For whom the Lord loveth he chasteneth, and scourgeth every son whom he receiveth. If ye endure chastening, God dealeth with you as with sons; for what son is he whom the father chasteneth not?

But continue thou in the things which thou hast learned, and hast been assured of, knowing of whom thou hast learned them.

By faith he (Moses) endured as seeing him who is invisible.

Thou therefore endure hardness as a good soldier of Jesus Christ.

He that shall endure unto the end, the same shall be saved.

EZEKIEL 22: 14
JAMES 1: 12
HEBREWS 12: 6-7
2 TIMOTHY 3: 14

HEBREWS 11: 27
2 TIMOTHY 2: 3
MARK 13: 13

MEDITATION

I am sure that you have often met the type of person who sets off with a great burst of enthusiasm on some project or other, but who often becomes disheartened or impatient when things do not turn out as he hoped. So it is in the Christian life. Many who showed great promise at the beginning have now turned aside because they found the way too hard. But our Lord never said it would be otherwise: 'If any man will come after me', says Christ, 'let him deny himself and take up his cross and follow me'. Now these things are not easy of attainment and if any of us have fallen by the wayside or turned aside from the path of duty, let us endeavour by his grace to take up our cross today and follow him, remembering that 'he who endureth unto the end shall be saved'.

Our souls we know when He appears
Shall bear His image bright;
For all His glory full disclosed
Shall open to our sight.

A hope so great and so divine
May trials well endure;
And purge the soul from sense and sin
As Christ Himself is pure.

PRAYER

Thou knowest O Lord how faint-hearted and discouraged we often become as we journey along the perplexing pathway of life. Give unto us we pray that spirit of endurance which shall make us strong in the hour of temptation and enable us to prevail in times of trial so that by Thy grace we may go onward until our journeying days are done. And this we ask for Jesus' sake.

AMEN.

23

Confidence

READING

O Lord, my hope and confidence
Is placed in thee alone;
Then let thy servant never be
Put to confusion.

It is better to trust in the Lord than to put confidence in man. It is better to trust in the Lord than to put confidence in princes.

Blessed is the man whom thou choosest and causest to approach unto thee, that he may dwell in thy courts: who art the confidence of all the ends of the earth, and of them that are far off upon the sea.

For the Lord shall be thy confidence and shall keep thy foot from being taken.

In the fear of the Lord is strong confidence: And his children shall have a place of refuge.

In returning and rest shall ye be saved; in quietness and in confidence shall be your strength.

And this is the confidence that we have in him, that, if we ask anything according to his will he heareth us.

And now little children, abide in him; that, when he shall appear, we may have confidence, and not be ashamed before him at his coming.

PSALM 118: 8-9	ISAIAH 30 15
PSALM 65: 4-5	1 JOHN 5: 14
PROVERBS 3: 26	1 JOHN 2: 28
PROVERBS 14: 26	

MEDITATION

Life becomes much easier and more serene when we have confidence in our fellow men. Thus, for example, if I have confidence in the driver of the car in which I am travelling I enjoy the outing much more. In like manner, if I have confidence in my doctor, I feel that I can safely entrust myself to his care and follow his advice. If this holds true in the physical realm it is equally true in the spiritual, for if I believe that God is working out His purposes in my life then I am confident that all the experiences through which I pass are part of His plan, whereby, even though I cannot understand it at the time. He brings blessings in disguise. Such an attitude of mind throws a new light on suffering and trial and it reminds us that 'while no chastening for the present seemeth to be joyous but grievous nevertheless afterwards it yieldeth the peaceable fruits of righteousness to them that are exercised thereby'.

Rock of ages cleft for me,
Let me hide myself in Thee,
Let the water and the blood,
From Thy riven side which flowed,
Be of sin the double cure,
Cleanse me from its guilt and power.

PRAYER

Our gracious God and Father in heaven, Thou knowest the doubts and fears which arise in our minds from time to time which cause us to lose confidence both in ourselves and in Thee. Increase our faith O Lord so that with renewed hope and confidence we may rest in Thy promises and feel assured that Thou art with us at all times and in all circumstances. We ask this in the name and for the sake of Christ our Saviour.

AMEN.

24

Protection

READING

The Lord's my light and saving health,
Who shall make me dismayed?
My life's strength is the Lord, of whom
Then shall I be afraid.

Keep me as the apple of the eye, hide me under the shadow of thy wings, from the wicked that oppress me, from my deadly enemies who compass me about.

Keep back thy servant also from presumptuous sins; let them not have dominion over me.

Set a watch, O Lord, before my mouth; keep the door of my lips.

I am with thee, and will keep thee in all places whither thou goest.

The Lord is thy keeper; the Lord is thy shade upon thy right hand. The Lord shall preserve thee from all evil; he shall preserve thy soul. The Lord shall preserve thy going out and thy coming in from this time forth, and even for evermore.

For he shall give his angels charge over thee, to keep thee in all thy ways. They shall bear thee up in their hands, lest thou dash thy foot against a stone.

Psalm 17: 8-9	Genesis 28: 15
Psalm 19: 13	Psalm 121: 5, 7 and 8
Psalm 141: 3	Psalm 91: 11-12

MEDITATION

It is a humbling thought, but none the less a true one that man needs to be kept. He is continually exposed not only to physical dangers, but also to moral danger and no matter how confident he may feel the fact remains that if left to himself he will fall. The Psalmist knew from bitter experience how liable he was to err and so he prayed, 'keep back thy servant from presumptuous sins'. He knew also that life was beset with physical dangers and so we find him praying, 'keep me as the apple of the eye'. If the Psalmist felt his need to pray in this fashion so should we, for we are exposed to the same dangers and temptations as he was. So let us lift up our hearts anew to God today and ask him to keep us strong in faith and ever walking on the road that leadeth Heavenwards.

Thy full protection Lord we claim
For all Thy promises are sure;
Thy children never ask in vain
But know, in Thee, they are secure.

PRAYER

O Lord our God whose strong arm is always ready to protect Thy children, help us to remember the dangers, both physical and moral to which we are exposed each day. Protect us we beseech of Thee from all harm and danger; make us strong in the hour of temptation and enable us to have the victory over self and over sin so that we may not dishonour the name of our Lord and Saviour.

AMEN.

The Heavenly Guide

READING

I will instruct thee and thee teach
The way that thou shalt go;
And with mine eye upon thee set,
I will direction show.

O send out thy light and thy truth; let them lead me; let them bring me unto thy holy hill, and to thy tabernacles.

Search me O God and know my heart; try me and know my thoughts; and see if there be any wicked way in me, and lead me in the way everlasting.

Good and upright is the Lord; therefore will he teach sinners in the way. The meek will he guide in judgment and the meek will he teach his way.

I have yet many things to say unto you, but ye cannot bear them now. Howbeit when the Spirit of truth is come, he will guide you into all truth; for he shall not speak of himself; but whatsoever he shall hear that shall he speak; and he will shew you things to come.

Nevertheless I am continually with thee, thou hast holden me by thy right hand. Thou shalt guide me with thy counsel and afterward receive me to glory.

For this God is our God for ever and ever; he will be our guide even unto death.

Psalm 43: 3	John 16: 12-13
Psalm 139: 23-24	Psalm 73: 23-24
Psalm 25: 8-9	Psalm 48: 14

MEDITATION

As we journey along the road of life it is so easy to take a wrong turning and, as the Psalmist says 'stray out of those ways of thine'. The way which we take may appear to be perfectly right in our own eyes, but it is often a path which leads us away from God. 'There is a way', says the wise man, 'that seemeth right unto a man but the end thereof is death'. Thus it is evident that we need a guide and God has promised by His Word and by His Spirit to guide us into all truth. Let us not be so foolish then as to think that we can guide ourselves, but let us take the Bible as our text book remembering that it is 'a lamp unto our feet and a light unto our path' and seeking the enlightenment of God's Spirit may we be enabled to walk on the straight and narrow path which leadeth unto life.

Walk in the light, and thou shalt know
That fellowship of love
His Spirit only can bestow
Who reigns in light above.

Walk in the light and thine shall be
A path, though thorny, bright
For God, by grace, shall dwell in thee
And God himself is light.

PRAYER

O Lord, we confess with shame that we are so prone to follow the path of our own choosing and stray from the strait and narrow path which leadeth unto life. We pray that Thou wilt guide us by Thy counsel so that we may ever walk on the road which leadeth heavenward and journey ever onward in Thy strength and by Thy grace until we reach the Father's home, through Jesus Christ our Lord.

AMEN.

26

The Light of the World

READING

O send thy light forth and thy truth;
Let them be guides to me,
And bring me to thy holy hill,
Ev'n where thy dwellings be.

The Lord is my light and my salvation; whom shall I fear? the Lord is the strength of my life; of whom shall I be afraid?

For God who commanded the light to shine out of darkness, hath shined in our hearts, to give the light of the knowledge of the glory of God in the face of Jesus Christ.

Then spake Jesus again unto them saying, I am the light of the world: he that followeth me shall not walk in darkness but shall have the light of life.

Ye are the light of the world. A city that is set on an hill cannot be hid.

Let your light so shine before men, that they may see your good works, and glorify your Father which is in heaven.

PSALM 27: 1   JOHN 8: 12
2 CORINTHIANS 4: 6   MATTHEW 5: 14, 16

MEDITATION

Every traveller needs light as he journeys along the road of life—he needs light on the path which lies ahead and light on the problems which confront him. It is not surprising, therefore, to find the Psalmist praying for guidance in these words, 'O send out thy light and thy truth: let them lead me'.

It is well for us to remember, however, that the Christian not only requires light but should also radiate light, for Christ said to his disciples, 'You are the light of the world'. Now it is not always easy to radiate light, especially in times of pain and weakness; yet how many there are who, even when walking in the shadow, have been able to reflect the light which is in Christ, and, because of this, others have been cheered and helped on their way. Let us endeavour then by God's grace to let our light so shine that some may have reason to thank God for our witness and have their eyes directed towards Him who is the Light of the World.

> *O Light, that followest all my way,*
> *I yield my flickering torch to Thee;*
> *My heart restores its borrowed ray,*
> *That in Thy sunshine blaze its day*
> *May brighter, fairer be.*

PRAYER

O Thou who of old commanded the light to shine out of darkness we pray Thee to shine into our hearts today dispelling our doubts and our fears and enabling us to bask in the sunshine of Thy love. As we come in contact with others help us to reflect that light in our lives so that they may see in us something of the beauty of Jesus and be attracted to Him, in whose name we ask this.

Amen.

The Storms of Life

READING

The storm is changed into a calm
At his command and will;
So that the waves, which raged before
Now quiet are and still.

But now thus saith the Lord that created thee, O Jacob, and he that formed thee, O Israel, Fear not: for I have redeemed thee, I have called thee by thy name; thou art mine. When thou passest through the waters, I will be with thee, and through the rivers, they shall not overflow thee: when thou walkest through the fire, thou shall not be burned; neither shall the flame kindle upon thee.

For I am persuaded, that neither death, nor life; nor angels, nor principalities, nor powers, nor things present, nor things to come, nor height nor depth, nor any other creature, shall be able to separate us from the love of God, which is in Christ Jesus our Lord.

And he saw them toiling in rowing; for the wind was contrary unto them; and about the fourth watch of the night he cometh unto them, walking upon the sea, and would have passed by them. For they all saw him and were troubled. And immediately he talked with them, and saith unto them, Be of good cheer: it is I; be not afraid. And he went up unto them into the ship, and the wind ceased.

ISAIAH 43: 1-2   MARK 6: 48, 50, 51
ROMANS 8: 38-39

MEDITATION

It is when we pass through the most difficult experiences in life that we are most conscious of our need of a friend and it is at such moments that the Heavenly Friend makes His Presence felt in a very real way, for He is the One who has said, 'When thou passest through the waters I will be with thee, and through the rivers they shall not overflow thee' and His promise never fails. Unfortunately, however, like the disciples in the ship we do not always recognise Him when our frail bark is tossed on stormy waters, and when we see Him we are afraid. Let us pray then that amidst the storms of life we may ever remember that Jesus Christ is the Master of the storm and when He comes to us walking on the billows may we gladly welcome Him aboard and hear His voice say to us, 'Be of good cheer: it is I; be not afraid'.

Jesu, Lover of my soul,
Let me to Thy bosom fly,
While the nearer waters roll,
While the tempest still is high;
Hide me, O my Saviour, hide
Till the storm of life be past;
Safe into the haven guide;
O receive my soul at last!

PRAYER

O Lord God when the storms of life threaten to engulf us as we voyage through time to eternity may we remember that He who stilled the storm on Galilee is still the same and that He is able to calm our troubled hearts. We ask that we may trust Him at all times remembering that He alone is able to pilot our frail craft through the stormy waters and bring us at last to our desired haven. Hear this our prayer for His name's sake.

AMEN.

28

Holiness

READING

Thy testimonies every one
In faithfulness excel;
And holiness for ever Lord,
Thine house becometh well.

Holy, holy, holy, Lord God Almighty, which was, and is, and is to come, Thou art worthy O Lord to receive glory and honour and power; for thou hast created all things, and for thy pleasure they are and were created.

There is none holy as the Lord; for there is none beside thee; neither is there any rock like our God.

Thou art holy, O thou that inhabitest the praises of Israel. Our fathers trusted in thee; they trusted and thou didst deliver them.

Who shall not fear thee O Lord, and glorify thy name? for thou only art holy; for all nations shall come and worship before thee; for thy judgments are made manifest.

But as he which hath called you is holy, so ye be holy in all manner of conversation; because it is written, Be ye holy, for I am holy.

He (chastened us) for our profit, that we might be partakers of his holiness. Follow peace with all men, and holiness, without which no man shall see the Lord.

REVELATION 4: 8 and 11   REVELATION 15: 4
1 SAMUEL 2: 2   1 PETER 1: 15-16
PSALM 22: 3-4   HEBREWS 12: 10, 14

MEDITATION

God and man are poles apart by reason of the fact that God is holy and man is sinful. Sin has separated us from God and consequently man cannot even contemplate the holiness of God; in fact when he attempts to do so he finds himself out of his depth. Yet we have just read—He chastened us for our profit 'that we might be partakers of his holiness'. Now that throws an entirely new light on pain and suffering doesn't it? God is not being unkind when He permits illness; it is for our profit that we might be 'partakers of his holiness'. It is often in the hour of illness that the Holy Spirit, who is the author of holiness, enlightens our minds so that we realise how neglectful of God we have been. Let us ever be willing then to submit to His discipline and may the mysterious dispensations of Providence be for our good so that there may be in our lives 'fruit unto holiness and the end everlasting life'.

Finish then Thy new creation:
Pure and spotless let it be;
Let us see Thy great salvation,
Perfectly restored in Thee,
Changed from glory into glory,
Till in heaven we take our place,
Till we cast our crowns before Thee,
Lost in wonder, love and praise.

PRAYER

O Lord most high and most holy who cannot look upon sin, we realise that our sins have separated us from Thee, but we thank Thee for Him who is the Mediator, even Jesus Christ Thy Son our Lord and Saviour, and we pray that He will cleanse us from all sin, so that wearing the spotless robe of His righteousness we may be accepted as holy in Thy sight, through Jesus Christ our Lord.

AMEN.

29

Power

The glory of thy kingdom show
Shall they, and of thy power tell:
That so men's sons his deeds may know,
His Kingdom's grace that doth excel.

Wherefore David blessed the Lord before all the congregation; and David said, Blessed be thou Lord God of Israel our father, for ever and ever. Thine O Lord is the greatness, and the power, and the glory, and the victory, and the majesty; for all that is in the heaven and the earth is thine.

Hast thou not known? has thou not heard, that the everlasting God the Lord, the Creator of the ends of the earth fainteth not, neither is weary? there is no searching of his understanding; He giveth power to the faint and to them that have no might he increaseth strength.

Touching the Almighty we cannot find him out; he is excellent in power, and in judgment, and in plenty of justice; he will not afflict. Men do therefore fear him; he respecteth not any that are wise of heart.

God hath spoken once; twice have I heard this; that power belongeth unto God. Also unto thee O Lord belongeth mercy for thou renderest to every man according to his work.

And Jesus came and spake unto them, saying, All power is given unto me in heaven and in earth. Go ye therefore and teach all nations baptizing them in the name of the Father, and of the Son, and of the Holy Ghost.

1 CHRONICLES 29: 10-11   PSALM 62: 11-12
ISAIAH 40: 28-29   MATTHEW 28: 18-19
JOB 37: 23-24

MEDITATION

We are often guilty of seeking to bring God down to our level, but when we do that we rob Him of His power and He ceases to be God. God has manifested His power in creation and in redemption—His is

> the power by which our Saviour rose,
> victorious o'er the grave.

In the days of his flesh Jesus Christ ministered unto the needs of the sick and 'His touch has still its ancient power'. He is the Good Physician, the One 'from whom all skill and science flow'. Let us not be ashamed then to recognise our need of His healing touch and may His power be made manifest not only in the healing of our bodies, but also of our souls.

> *Jesus, my all in all Thou art,*
> *My rest in toil, mine ease in pain;*
> *The medicine of my broken heart;*
> *In war my peace; in loss my gain:*
> *My smile beneath the tyrants frown;*
> *In shame my glory and my crown.*

PRAYER

Almighty and all powerful God who during the days of Thy flesh didst manifest Thy power in so many different ways; we thank Thee especially today for that power by which the Saviour triumphed over death and for the blessed hope which comes to us through His resurrection. May that hope be ours today and that power be made manifest in our lives so that we may have the victory in Thy great name.

AMEN.

30

Patience

READING

I waited for the Lord my God,
And patiently did bear;
At length to me He did incline
My voice and cry to hear.

Better is the end of a thing than the beginning thereof; and the patient in spirit is better than the proud in spirit.

For what glory is it, if when ye be buffeted for your faults ye shall take it patiently? but if when ye do well, and suffer for it ye take it patiently, this is acceptable with God. For even hereunto were ye called; because Christ also suffered for us, leaving us an example, that ye should follow his steps.

Be patient therefore brethren into the coming of the Lord, Behold the husbandman waiteth for the precious fruit of the earth, and hath long patience for it, until he receive the early and latter rain. Be ye also patient; stablish your hearts: for the coming of the Lord draweth nigh.

Wherefore . . . let us lay aside every weight, and the sin which doth so easily beset us, and let us run with patience the race that is set before us, looking unto Jesus, the author and finisher of our faith.

Now the God of patience and consolation grant you to be likeminded one toward another according to Christ Jesus.

ECCLESIASTES 7: 8   HEBREWS 12: 1-2
1 PETER 2: 20-21   ROMANS 15: 5-6
JAMES 5: 7-8

MEDITATION

The grace of patience is one of the most winsome of all
Christian graces, but it is not easy to attain. We find it so
easy to be impatient when the least little speck appears to
cloud our horizon and when we find ourselves beset with
trouble and difficulty then we immediately begin to find
fault with God. The writer to the Hebrews says 'ye have
need of patience that after ye have done the will of God ye
might receive the promise'. What is God's will for us? God
we are told 'is not willing that any should perish, but that
all should come to everlasting life'. Again we are told 'this
is the will of God even your sanctification'. So let us,
asking God's help to acquiesce in His will, 'lay aside every
weight and the sin which doth so easily beset us and run
with patience the race which is set before us looking unto
Jesus'.

Rest of the weary, Joy of the sad,
Hope of the dreary, Light of the glad,
Home of the stranger, Strength to the end,
Refuge from danger, Saviour and Friend.

PRAYER

O Lord we confess that often we become impatient,
especially in times of sickness and adversity and so we
pray for the grace of patience today. May we see Thy hand
at work in all the vicissitudes of life and ever remember
that all things—even the unpleasant things in life—'work
together for good to them that love God'. Help us
therefore to exercise patience in the spirit of expectancy
believing that 'the coming of the Lord draweth nigh'. We
ask this in the Saviour's name.

AMEN.

31

Perfection

READING

Mark thou the perfect, and behold
The man of uprightness;
Because that surely of this man
The latter end is peace.

Be ye therefore perfect, even as your Father which is in heaven is perfect.

Jesus said unto him, If thou wilt be perfect, go and sell that thou hast, and give to the poor and thou shalt have treasure in heaven, and come follow me.

For it became him, for whom are all things and by whom are all things, in bringing many sons unto glory, to make the captain of their salvation perfect through sufferings.

Therefore leaving the principles of the doctrine of Christ, let us go on unto perfection; not laying again the foundation of repentance from dead works, and of faith toward God.

Now the God of peace that brought again from the dead our Lord Jesus, that great shepherd of the sheep, through the blood of the everlasting covenant, make you perfect in every good work to do his will, working in you that which is well pleasing in his sight, through Jesus Christ; to whom be glory for ever and ever. Amen.

MATTHEW 5: 48   HEBREWS 6: 1
MATTHEW 19: 21   HEBREWS 13: 20-21
HEBREWS 2: 10

MEDITATION

I am quite sure that none of us has ever met a perfect man, for the simple reason that even the best and most saintly men who have ever lived have all had some imperfection: 'There is none righteous', saith the Lord, 'no not one'. Yet perfection is the goal which is held out to us in Scripture: 'Be ye therefore perfect, even as your Father in Heaven is perfect'. How is this goal to be achieved? It is to be achieved through the gracious operation of the Holy Spirit who enables us not only to open our hearts to receive Jesus Christ but also (to quote the words of the Westminster Shorter Catechism) 'enables us more and more to die unto sin and live unto righteousness'. Final perfection is not reached in this life but as we trust in God, so help us to go from strength to strength until at length perfect we appear before Him.

> *O may Thy Spirit seal our souls*
> *And mould them to Thy will,*
> *That our weak hearts no more may stray*
> *But keep Thy precepts still;*
> *That to perfection's sacred height*
> *We nearer still may rise;*
> *And all we think, and all we do,*
> *Be pleasing in Thine eyes.*

PRAYER

Most gracious God, as we think of the many blemishes in our lives we realise that of ourselves we can never attain to that standard of perfection which Thou dost demand of us. So we ask that through the gracious operation of the Holy Spirit working within us we may be enabled 'more and more to die unto sin and to live unto righteousness'. Grant we beseech of Thee that when our travelling days are done we may appear perfect before Thee without spot or blemish and sing Thy praises throughout the countless ages of eternity.

AMEN.